Book by Book

—

A BIBLE STUDY COMPANION FROM
THE DAILY GRACE CO.

THE DAILY GRACE CO.

Book of the Bible:

_____

Date of Study:

_____ _____

Prayer

Apart from the Holy Spirit, the Word of God would fall
on deaf ears. It is through the work of the Holy Spirit
alone that we can understand the glorious truths of
Scripture and be transformed by it.

*Use the space below to write a prayer asking God to
bring about knowledge, understanding, and
real change as you study His Word.*

Background Information

Before studying any book of the Bible, it is worthwhile to gather background information in order to understand the historical context in which the book was written. Some information can be found in the text itself, while other information will require the use of commentaries or other resources. One good place to find this information is in the introduction to each book of the Bible in the ESV Study Bible.

In your reading, try to answer the following archaeological questions:

AUTHOR

Who wrote the book? _____

_____

What information do you know about the author from the text itself? _____

_____

_____

_____

_____

_____

_____

_____

_____

_____

_____

What additional information about the author can you gather from study Bibles and commentaries? _____

_____

_____

_____

_____

_____

_____

_____

_____

_____

_____

How does the information about the author impact the way you read the book? _____

_____

_____

_____

_____

_____

_____

_____

_____

_____

_____

_____

_____

AUDIENCE

Who was this book written to? _____

_____

_____

What information do you know about the audience from the
text itself? _____

_____

_____

_____

_____

_____

_____

_____

_____

_____

What additional information about the audience can you
gather from study Bibles and commentaries? _____

_____

_____

_____

_____

_____

_____

_____

_____

How does the information about the author impact the way you read the book? _____

_____

_____

_____

_____

_____

_____

_____

_____

_____

_____

_____

_____

DATE

When was the book written? _____

What important historical events might impact the way you understand the book? _____

_____

_____

_____

_____

_____

_____

_____

_____

PURPOSE

What is the author's purpose in writing this book? _____

_____

_____

_____

_____

_____

_____

_____

_____

_____

_____

_____

How does the purpose impact the way you read the book?

_____

_____

_____

_____

_____

_____

_____

_____

_____

_____

_____

GENRE

What is the genre of the book? _____

_____

What are some characteristics of this genre? _____

_____

_____

_____

_____

_____

_____

_____

_____

How does the genre impact the way you read the book?

_____

_____

_____

_____

_____

_____

_____

_____

_____

_____

_____

_____

HISTORICAL CONTEXT

What is the cultural and historical climate of the time?

_____

_____

_____

_____

_____

_____

_____

_____

_____

_____

How does the context inform the meaning of the book?

_____

_____

_____

_____

_____

_____

_____

_____

_____

_____

_____

BIBLICAL CONTEXT

How does this book fit in the biblical narrative? _____

_____

_____

_____

_____

_____

_____

What citations/allusions or historical connections to other
books is the author making? _____

_____

_____

_____

_____

_____

_____

What biblical theology themes emerge from this text that are
present throughout Scripture? _____

_____

_____

_____

_____

_____

_____

Outline

Read the book from start to finish at least once, then use the
space provided to outline the contents of the book.

Themes

Use the space provided to note key themes that
you observe as you study.

_____

_____

_____

_____

_____

_____

_____

_____

_____

_____

_____

_____

_____

_____

_____

_____

_____

_____

_____

_____

_____

_____

_____

_____

SHIFTS, TRANSITIONS, & BREAKS

What shifts, transitions, or breaks are in the text?
If needed, refer to the Transition Words reference list on page 42.

REPEATED WORDS & PHRASES

What repeated words and phrases do you see in the book?

THE GOSPEL

How does this book connect to the gospel? _____

_____

_____

_____

_____

_____

_____

_____

_____

_____

_____

_____

What aspects of the gospel are highlighted in this book?

_____

_____

_____

_____

_____

_____

_____

_____

_____

_____

_____

_____

How does this book of the Bible point to Christ? _____

_____

_____

_____

_____

_____

_____

_____

_____

_____

_____

_____

Does it speak explicitly of Jesus? _____

_____

_____

_____

_____

_____

_____

_____

_____

_____

_____

_____

Are there aspects of typology? _____

_____

_____

_____

_____

_____

_____

_____

_____

_____

_____

_____

Are there messianic prophecies? _____

_____

_____

_____

_____

_____

_____

_____

_____

_____

_____

_____

Does the passage highlight the need for a Messiah? _____

_____

_____

_____

_____

_____

_____

_____

_____

_____

_____

_____

_____

How is Jesus the answer to the problems presented in the book?

_____

_____

_____

_____

_____

_____

_____

_____

_____

_____

_____

_____

Character of God

What does this book reveal about God and His character?
If needed, refer to the Attributes of God reference list on page 43.

_____

_____

_____

_____

_____

_____

_____

_____

_____

_____

_____

_____

_____

_____

_____

_____

_____

_____

_____

_____

_____

_____

Application

Write specific and practical application points based on the text, and then answer the application questions on the next page.

_____

_____

_____

_____

_____

_____

_____

_____

_____

_____

_____

_____

_____

_____

_____

_____

_____

_____

_____

_____

_____

_____

_____

_____

_____

_____

APPLICATION QUESTIONS

Are there sins to flee from in this book? _____

_____

_____

_____

_____

_____

_____

_____

_____

_____

_____

Are there commands to obey in this book? _____

_____

_____

_____

_____

_____

_____

_____

_____

_____

_____

_____

_____

Are there actions or attitudes to emulate in this book? _____

_____

_____

_____

_____

_____

_____

_____

_____

_____

_____

_____

_____

Are there principles to follow in this book? _____

_____

_____

_____

_____

_____

_____

_____

_____

_____

_____

_____

How does this text remind me of my fallen condition? _____

_____
_____
_____
_____
_____
_____
_____
_____
_____

How should the truth of who God is as revealed in this text
change the way I live? _____

_____
_____
_____
_____
_____
_____
_____
_____
_____
_____
_____

How should what I have learned about God change my heart
and attitude toward my circumstances? _____

_____

_____

_____

_____

_____

_____

_____

_____

_____

What practical things can I do in light of this passage? _____

_____

_____

_____

_____

_____

_____

_____

_____

_____

_____

_____

_____

_____

Encouraging Verses

Write down any verses that are particularly encouraging
to you as you study.

Praying Scripture

God speaks to us through His Word, and we respond to Him in prayer. Studying God's Word should not be merely an intellectual exercise but a practice that engages both our heads and our hearts. Therefore, our study of Scripture should always be saturated in prayer from start to finish, and we should respond to what God has revealed to us by praying to Him.

Not only can we pray in response to God's Word, but we can also pray the very words of Scripture back to God. Many parts of Scripture contain prayers that we can pray directly. Even parts of Scripture that are not explicitly written as prayers can serve to give words to our petitions.

As you study, write down verses that you can pray for yourself or for others.

Biggest Takeaway

What are the biggest takeaways after reading this book?

_____

_____

_____

_____

_____

_____

_____

_____

_____

_____

_____

_____

_____

_____

_____

_____

_____

_____

_____

_____

_____

_____

Post Study Prayer

At the end of your book study, write a prayer using
the following prompts:

Adoration & Thanksgiving

Praise God for who He is and what He has done
as revealed in this book.

Confession

Confess the sins that this book has exposed in your own
life, and ask for forgiveness. Ask God to help you put
those sins to death.

Supplication

Ask God to help you follow the commands He has given
in this book. Ask Him to transform your heart. Pray the
truths of Scripture for others who come to mind and
for the church as a whole.

_____

_____

_____

_____

_____

_____

_____

_____

_____

_____

_____

Notes

TRANSITION WORDS REFERENCE LIST

USED TO SHOW:	EXAMPLES:
Emphasis	*importantly, absolutely, in particular, it should be noted, etc.*
Addition	*furthermore, also, to, along with, moreover, but also, etc.*
Contrast	*nevertheless, despite, in contrast to, while, where as, even so, etc.*
Order	*first or firstly, before, subsequently, above all, following, first and foremost, etc.*
Result	*therefore, thus, hence, for this reason, due to, etc.*
Illustration	*for example, such as, including, namely, like, etc.*
Comparison	*similarly, likewise, just as, in the same way, etc.*
Summary	*in conclusion, altogether, etc.*
Reason	*because of, with this in mind, in fact, in order to, due to, etc.*
Condition	*if, in case, unless, etc.*
Concession	*admittedly, even so, although, even though, however, etc.*

ATTRIBUTES OF GOD REFERENCE LIST

Eternal — God has no beginning and no end. He always was, always is, and always will be.

Faithful — God is incapable of anything but fidelity. He is loyally devoted to His plan and purpose.

Glorious — God is ultimately beautiful, deserving of all praise and honor.

Good — God is pure; there is no defilement in Him. He is unable to sin, and all He does is good.

Gracious — God is kind, giving to us gifts and benefits which we are undeserving of.

Holy — God is undefiled and unable to be in the presence of defilement. He is sacred and set-apart.

Immutable — God does not change. He is the same yesterday, today, and tomorrow.

Jealous — God is desirous of receiving the praise and affection He rightly deserves.

Just — God governs in perfect justice. He acts in accordance with justice. In Him there is no wrongdoing or dishonesty.

Love — God is eternally, enduringly, steadfastly loving and affectionate. He does not forsake or betray His covenant love.

Merciful — God is compassionate, withholding us from the wrath that we are deserving of.

Omnipotent — God is all-powerful; His strength is unlimited.

Omnipresent — God is everywhere; His presence is near and permeating.

Omniscient — God is all-knowing; there is nothing unknown to Him.

Patient — God is long-suffering and enduring. He gives ample opportunity for people to turn toward Him.

Righteous — God is blameless and upright. There is no wrong found in Him.

Sovereign — God governs over all things; He is in complete control.

True — God is our measurement of what is fact. By Him are we able to discern true and false.

Wise — God is infinitely knowledgeable and is judicious with His knowledge.

Thank you for studying
God's Word with us!

CONNECT WITH US

@thedailygraceco

@kristinschmucker

CONTACT US

info@thedailygraceco.com

SHARE

#thedailygraceco

#lampandlight

VISIT US ONLINE

thedailygraceco.com

MORE DAILY GRACE

The Daily Grace App

Daily Grace Podcast